Messages
From Absent Friends

Gill Pakes

Honeybee Books

Published by Honeybee Books
www.honeybeebooks.co.uk

Copyright Gill Pakes © 2022
Cover painting Copyright Sam Zambelli © 2022

The right of Gill Pakes to be identified as the author of this work has been asserted by her in accordance with the Copyright, Designs and Patents Act 1988.

No part of this book may be reproduced in any form or by any electronic or mechanical means including information storage and retrieval systems without permission in writing from the author.

Printed in the UK using paper from sustainable sources

ISBN: 978-1-913675-31-8

About the Author

I am a psychic medium, I have been doing card readings for over 30 years starting with family and friends. I have seen spirit from a young age and was often aware of my Nan sitting at the bottom of my bed. She died when I was two. In my 20s spirit was trying to contact me to work for them, but I was frightened and blocked them out.

My mum used to read playing cards; she was extremely accurate which frightened her, so she stopped doing them. My great aunt Lucy also used to read tea leaves, sadly I never knew her.

In my late 20's I met a lady who ran her own awareness group and invited me to join her. I've not looked back since.

I have gained a lot of experience over the years, spirit never fail to amaze me with the messages I give. I also do church services and run my own awareness group.

I'm now 64 and I'm still learning different ways of working with spirit. I always enjoy what I do and it's always good to find different ways of having contact with loved ones.

About this book

Sitting at home one day doing a lot of nothing, I had words pop into my head. I brushed them away but they were constant. I decided to write them down and when I read them back I was amazed to see it was a message in poem form. I put it on Facebook and was extremely surprised to have a lady contact me to say she understood every word I had written. I thought, ok just go with it. It wasn't long before I was given more words which I wrote down and again put them on Facebook to have people contact me saying thank you.

I meditated to ask who was giving me these beautiful, meaningful words. I was shocked when I heard the name of Ted Hughes. I had heard of him but didn't know much about him. I settled down to watch a documentary I had recorded a few weeks before and was blown away to see it was all about Ted Hughes and his late wife Sylvia. If that's not conformation I don't know what is. Since then Ted has given me the words for all my poems and I have learnt that his last book *Birthday Letters* were poems in story form from different parts of their lives. Spooky!

Contents

A Beaten Mother	1
A Good Night Ended Bad	2
A Loving Couple	3
A Special Bond	4
A Wedding Nightmare	5
Alzheimer's Dad	6
Aunties Grave	7
Bad Choices	8
Caring for Nan	9
Cheating Partner	10
Covid Death	11
Controlling Father	12
Dental Phobia	14
Depression	15
Divorce Party	16
Evil Father	17
Family Upset	18
Garden Buddies	19
Getting Better	20
Happy Holidays	21
Happy Memories	22
Haunted House	23
Hearty Affair	24
Holiday Hell	25
Ill and Alone	26
Isolation	27
Leaving Family Behind	28
Lifes Miseries	29
Making The Most of Life	30

My Friend	31
Our Special Bench	32
Parents Secret	33
Radio Listeners	34
Regrets	35
The Mother in Law	36
Uncertainty	37
Swimming Pool	38
Wonderful Mum	40

Messages
From Absent Friends

A Beaten Mother

Dorothy was her name
In all her glory to show
It's all on the outside
Her feelings are shown
Inside the house, behind closed doors
A different matter, not to be seen by all
The punches and the slaps
The verbal violation
Children are crying
With the sound at duration
When will it stop
I say to myself
Then a birth and a death
Answers that call
How things do change
The trousers have swapped
Now Dorothy is calling the shots
Behave or get out
She shouts with glee
Now peace is regained
In high society

A Good Night Ended Bad

Sitting up alone in my bed
Horrible thoughts going round in my head
My face is black n blue
Last night I lost my shoe
Meeting my friends
A good catch up is all in hand
A meal and some drinks
Life aint all that bad
We talked and laughed into the night
We fought back tears
Sometimes life is sad
And when it came to say goodnight
I lived so close, I walked so fast
Then out of the bushes he pounced
The deed was done and home I run
Back to my Mom and Dad
Secrets kept to myself

A Loving Couple

The skies are blue
And I am thinking of you
With all the fun times we had
Never a crossed word
And never a raised voice
Oh what a life we had
The holidays aboard the ships
The people that we met
No other couple were like us
In ways we like to share
The pyramids stood tall
Be careful dear, don't fall
Uneven ground is everywhere
We said as we flew home
Thank you again for a wonderful time
But lets just get back home
Our pride and joy in our castle
Is where I lay my head
I held your hand
And then I was dead

A Special Bond

Friends can be like sisters
When you have known them many years
The tears through fun and laughter
Are the tears of lots of joy
You're my special sister
Adopted one at that
One that's never forgotten
Can't say fairer than that
Be there for one another
Through the good times and the bad
You are my lovely sister
The one I never had
The holiday was fun you said
Hey lets go again
So passports bought
And money saved
Off to Benidorm and then
The memories that we share
The love we have between us
Is all stored up for future fun
No-one will come between us

A Wedding Nightmare

A day before my wedding
Is a day I'll never forget
The moment I had the phone call
Is a day of all regrets
The words that come
Went into space
I passed the phone
I was full of disgrace
It seems that I
Was living lie
To hear what bestowed on me
When there was love
To do this to someone
Who is now up above
The attack that I
Will never forget
And I myself
Will always regret

Alzheimer's Dad

It happened very gradually
I realise that now
The day I saw that somethings wrong
Was the day to start in hell
The missing shoe, the keys too
Your washing in the fridge
The T.V remote you swore was bespoke
And didn't work your T.V
Upside down, turn around
From the life you once had
The slaps that started
The anger too
It was getting really bad
You didn't know who I was by then
Getting you help was all I had
When they took you I broke down
I failed you I know
But you seemed to like
The people there
Someone new always there to talk too
Sleep well Dad

Aunties Grave

A visit to the graveyard
Was neither pleasant or nice
The bodies underground
Are the thoughts in my head
As I race over the ground
To the plot I need
Bunches of flowers
Are all strewn about
A rampage was here
By unworthy people
I start my clearance
On Aunties grave
To make it look tidy
Apart from her name
Next time I will bring
A paint pot and brush
To tidy the letters
I say with a huff
Now it's all done
I will be back next week
To keep it all tidy
Looking good neat and sleek
Amen

Bad Choices

Dave the rave, is here again
The names we used to call him
Women were his life and fun
Please don't ever stall him
He was not the marrying kind
He could never be tied down
To one woman all his life
The women they do swoon
And fall at his feet
But behind closed doors
They were just a piece of meat
The illness struck, Oh what a shock
He struggled even to put on a sock
Looking back on life
Now he's keen, to have and to hold
That special someone
Too little, too late

Caring for Nan

Oh Nan Oh Nan Oh Nan
Is how it all began
The day I became you're carer
I love you more each passing day
I'm happy to be near ya
The love you gave me
When I was only three
That time meant so much to me
My parents died, when I was five
Then you and Granddad stepped in
You looked after me
Like I was your own
Now it's my turn to look after you
The table has turned, I'm really concerned
You're weaker by the day
The time has come, to say goodbye
Goodbye but not forgotten

Cheating Partner

A mistake is made once
A mistake is made twice
Make the same mistake thrice
Don't ever come back again
A baby is born, but where are you
I've heard it all before
You stay at a mates house again
It wasn't until, I came home with a bundle
I find out the truth
A 'lady friend' you had that night
While I was giving birth
It's unforgivable, you're not the salt of the earth
Two times before a lady calls you
The excuses came thick and fast
The time has come to say goodbye
You will never break my heart again

Covid Death

I helped you after you'r husband died
We were just friends then
Everyone thought there was more to it
But we knew where we belonged
As the months passed by
And the years too
I started getting feelings for you
I knew you felt the same
But we wouldn't tell each other
Then the day came
It was a slip of the tongue you see
We made our feelings known
For all the world to see
We were happily married
A few years by then
When my health started to go
See the doctor you shouted in fright
But you know I wouldn't go
Then Covid hit, it hit me too
In my hospital bed I lay
You weren't allowed in to sit with me
All we could do was pray
But God above he needed me
To deliver milk bottles in the sky
I knew you were there
As my last breath was took
I know you're feeling bad
As I floated up above
I swore I would never leave you
As it stands as days go passed
My word is kept within you

Controlling Father

The days were long, the nights even longer
The trouble that's caused, it feels so stronger
Is my Father that bad, in my eyes he's not
I feel protected, no matter what
For everyone else, he's evil and bad
This thought makes me sad
The tears I've seen
Whose in the wrong here
I'm persuaded to go
With the wrong one, it's clear
At the time it seemed the right thing to do
I'm packing my bags then put on my shoe
A little time later I am looking around
People are missing
They are thin on the ground
Lets just see what lies ahead
I'm being told I've nothing to dread
I miss my Mom and my sisters too
Have I done the right thing, I'm feeling blue
I have chosen my life, there's no going back
My friends have all gone, my family too
So I understand why I am blue
It wasn't all bad but could have been better
The choices were made and I've found a letter
I sit and I read but I don't feel better
I shouldn't have seen this and I ask if there's more
I watch as the letters rattle through the door
They are taken swiftly, I'm not sure why
All I want to do is cry

When the time came when I wasn't my best
Alone in the hospital
I get it all off my chest
Staff don't believe me my Father don't care
Then as my eye's close I see a familiar face
No-one I've seen down here in this place
The face belongs to my family I see
A Grandmother figure is looking for me
I'm here Nan I cry out for her to see me
She then gives a shout, my dearest Emma
We meet at last
I know you've seen me, alone in you're past
I had gone before you were born
It doesn't mean I wasn't with you
When you were forlorn
I've bide my time, I've waited till now
We can be together all in the same place
Let's visit you're Mom you're sisters too
They will know we are here
They will find comfort too
I'm not gone I'm here by you're side
Promise me you make you're life as you want it
With out any strife
Think of me and I will be there
By your side, no time will be spared

Dental Phobia

Eating a lolly I chipped a tooth
Off to the dentist I go
Once I'm there I hide my face
The fear of the unknown
The dentist to me is mean and unkind
The dentist is stood beside me
Open wide he says with glee
Let me see what awaits me
My mouth opens slightly
He prods and pokes
Then he says with a smile
It's not as bad as you think
My mouth opens wider
He has a better look
All done now I hear him say
You're lucky you're off the hook
Off home I skip
With pleasure in my eyes
I've had such a lovely surprise

Depression

It's tea time again
What shall I cook today
Egg and chips or spag bol
Or something else I say
Day after day
It's always the same
What do I want to eat
The thoughts today
Are the same every day
Shall I skip a tea for sweets
It's monotonous and boring
No change at all to be had
As each day passes
The worse I get
I may as well give up now
Depression sets in
Start over, begin
I cook some chips
I'll have an egg with that too
I'm glad I've eaten
I was really hungry
What will tomorrow bring
It's the same day after day

Divorce Party

Christmas time is here at last
Now it's time to forget the past
All the woes and fears I've had
Now the fun and hope it lasts
My divorce is through
I'm glad to say
In the farmyard we made up in the hay
The last time ever
No more sex with you
It was all you were ever good at
The finger and thumbs
We rub our tums
At the feast before our eyes
We've all put in including the gin
The celebrations they do start
My divorce is here
It's all done and dusted it's clear
Raise a glass, let us cheer

Evil Father

Please don't lock me away
In the cupboard under the stairs
It's full of spiders, mice and hairs
It smells so bad, I feel sick
I'v done nothing wrong
Should I just quit
My Father tells me
I am so naughty
My punishment is dark and jaunty
Please let me out
I will be so good
My brother is like my Fatherhood
Let there be light, for me today
I sit and pray, pray, pray
Eventually I am released
I see mom deceased

Family Upset

Jelly and ice cream at Nannies for tea
Trifle a plenty but it's not for me
The cucumber sandwiches
Scattered around
The spam is also thick on the ground
The grown-ups they natter
I don't know what's said
And then Nan say's it's time for bed
I didn't know I was staying the night
Am I in trouble, I want my Mum
I don't understand what the hell's going on
Nan comes to see me
I can see the tears she's shed
She tries to assure me
I've got nothing to dread
I see my Mum the day after next
She tells me, be brave
For what I say next
My heart is breaking
My legs are like jelly
As I learn of the truth
There's lots there's plenty

Garden Buddies

Sitting in the garden
As beautiful as it is
It's much to big, for one to do
We did it together
When you was here
I miss you more
Each passing day
You're flying free you see
You left me oh so long ago
A replacement will never be
Arthur where are you my love
In my heart you'll always be
I'm sitting here, a slice of cake
Like we always did
You're special bench
You're names on there too
I know you're there, please wait for me
We'll be together for all time

Getting Better

I sit and think about you
You're always in my thoughts
The life you've had
Does not compare
To the road you should have walked
Bad decisions were made
But at the time were right
All you're life You've had to fight
The time is coming
The lights a spot
Plenty of time, you have got
Decisions are made
It's for the best you see
You're happiness means a lot to me
A magic wand, I wished I had
To wave across you
You're life turning less bad
My wishes for you
Is a happy healthy life
You are my friend, the love of my life

Happy Holidays

Let's go, let's go
There's no time to wait
The aircraft is landing
We will soon be boarding
And off we jolly well go
Off to Zante
Two years we have waited
For a holiday of this type
We are very lucky
To afford the luxury
Of a flight and hotel to boot
4 hours and 30 minutes will soon be gone
And into the sunshine
Our holidays anon
A fabulous time
We had while we were there
Ten days later, back we fly
Our cases jam packed
Lota of gifts we did buy
Can't wait to give them out
From our time by the sea

Happy Memories

Sitting in the sun
Is how the day begun
The birds are singing
The crickets are chirping
Oh what a wonderful time
September is close
And the nights are drawing in
Soon it will be snow
It will keep us all in
The fun to be is had
On the sledges and the skii's
Summers on it's way
I'm freezing my knees
As the days grow longer
And the suns warming up
Holiday to plan
I won't go in the buff
Out of all the seasons
Spring is the best
All the life of the plants
And the new borns rear their heads
Spring, summer and autumn too
The winter snow will soon be back
Wrap up stay warm
Don't get a chill

Haunted House

Sitting in the lounge
On Rotherfield Road
Round comes my neighbour
She keeps me on my toes
What shall we do
We both say in unison
We make a telling board
And start playing hard
What follows next
Will never be repeated
The glass moves on it's own
Were there any preachers
Then we hear the noises
Followed by the voices
We are both screaming
Let's get out right now
We were both in pieces
Throwing away all the letters
Washing the glass it smashes into pieces
The house after that
Never felt safe
And many a time
There were faces in the grate
Footsteps above, the bedrooms are noisy
Not fit to be slept in
But no chance at the time, I'm glad I have left
To leave it all behind

Hearty Affair

As soon as my eyes set on you
You were all I could think of
The joys we shared, were never compared
To any other I met
From my pants to my tea
You were always with me
My saviour I know you were
If only I wasn't married then
I know you would be my wife
So many obstacles
Most of which I could have changed
To have you fully in my life
I would do it all again
The healing given by both of us
To others and ourselves
Unfortunate times there are to come
When my heart will no longer beat
I will always wait for you my dear
No other will compete

Holiday Hell

With a brochure in my hands
I sit and read
The seas and the beaches
Are calling to me
As discussions take place
With all involved
The final destination
To love and to hold
Excited we become
As we settle on a place
The packing takes place
The control is all mine
Our holiday will be divine
Half way through the news is bad
We've only been here for a very short time
He's taken ill, no time to rest
An ambulance is called
The time is of the essence
Too late, no time left
Saying goodbye is the worse yet

Ill and Alone

I woke up this morning
Happy and full of beans
The doctor will see me
And then I started to sneeze
A trip up to the docs
I will be better soon
But what he says to me
Fills my soul with doom
I hear the words
But don't listen to what's said
The results are back
Unexpected as they are
I think this test is a test too far
I didn't want to know
I've not much time left
I tell my family
But they don't seem concerned
Now I know I'm suffering alone
I hope they can forgive themselves

Isolation

Sitting quiet on the stairs
No one's here
No one stares
What am I thinking
I don't know
I didn't know yesterday
I still don't know today
Will I ever know what happiness is
Yes of course I do anyway
I am so happy
I am so well
Look inside see how I dwell
You cannot see me
You cannot say
All the love
Is coming your way
I'm still with you
Take my blessings every day

Leaving Family Behind

As the foggy night is lifted
I see you standing there
The boy with the light brown hair
My heart is fluttering
I know yours is too
Are we soul mates, me and you
We get together
Upset are some
But look at us now
How far we have come
No -one would guess
We have love like ours
I pray each night, upon the stars
We will be together, for all our days
We are both sure, this is the only way

Lifes Miseries

A happy ever after
Has always been for me
I must have been dreaming
At all the things that's happened to be
All doom and gloom
And tears and sorrow
Right up to today and tomorrow
In love I pick badly
Things don't go my way
My work and home life too
It's like living in hell
The tears I have shed
It won't end well
At last some salvation
When I'm told the news
My boss has moved on
My husband is dead
Now I can sleep soundly
Alone in my bed

Making The Most of Life

In a hospital bed
I sit and wait
After months of pain
I will hear my fate
The doctor comes
All smiles is he
He's got good news
Me thinks it's for me
And so it seems
That I was right
I'm packing my stuff
To set off in the night
Away I go
To my home after weeks
And to spread the good news
To all that like me
The day after
A party is sought
To celebrate more
Time that I'm bought

My Friend

A friend like you
Is always true
You stand there by my side
My right and my wrongs
You never take sides
You're there for me
At all times
Grateful I will always be
For a friend like you
Looking out for me
Right from the other side

Our Special Bench

On our special bench
I sit and wait
For the time, we can meet again
I feel it will be sooner
And definitely not later
Oh look the tides coming in
We used to sit
And eat fish and chips
Here on this bench
The laughs we had
It wasn't all bad
We will meet again
I wait for my time
I hope it won't be long
I miss you loads
You're warts n all
The rows we had
Have gone to the light
Right now, I'm losing the fight
Not long now, I can see
Before you come, to meet me

Parents Secret

Visiting my parents
The house was full of joy
As always, it's nice to see
But somethings not quite right
For all the world to see
Asking one then the other
Both their heads said no
Nothing wrong or amiss
Gosh they are so strong
Weeks rolled on, going into months
The day had finally come
My hell had just begun
I'm told the fate of my dearest Dad
He's not got long to live
The cancers spreading amongst the bones
He now lives in fear and dread
I'm so sorry I heard him say
We didn't want you worrying
Please don't be mad and don't be sad
I can't cope with that as well
As I sit there emotions rolling
I can only answer in my head
I'm really angry and then I'm sad
For what they've kept from me
There's no turning back
And forward has stopped
In limbo they do find me
Only days later, the phone call comes
The end is here the day is done
Home I go just with my Mum

Radio Listeners

Listening to the radio
Is what we used to do
Every day we were together
Was a blessing in disguise
Every time we looked at each other
We'd become bleary eyed
The love we had
Could not compare at all
To anyone around us
We could stand tall
The radio kept us sane
We sang along with the tunes
We laughed at each other
It wasn't against the rules
And now your gone
And I'm still here
Our favourite songs
Are still ringing in my ear
Gone but not forgotten
I now sing for both of us
The wind beneath my wings

Regrets

That day in December
I will always remember
The row we sat and had
I stormed out that day
Never to return
I sat and cried
Tears rolling down my eyes
And then I started to think
The more I thought how daft it was
To be so angry with each other
I drove home quick
But it was too late
I hope his dying was quick
He had took his life
And left a note
A cross I will have to bare
Lots of regrets fill my head
I'm going crazy locking myself inside
You are my one and only love

The Mother in Law

The Mother in Law
Well what can I say
She ruled the roost, she ruled our lives
And ruled our kids beside
All our holidays were planned out as well
The regimentation all through the week
Caused my head to swell
It's not right, it's not fair
The beach is out of bounds
It's not what they want to do
So the kids they suffered
All because of you
Our holidays were spoilt
They were just like a visit
Until we walked away
Things thank God
Will never be the same
Things are much better now

Uncertainty

The t.v is on, I hear no words
My mind is blank
There is no verse
The language that's spoken
I don't understand
My mind is in turmoil
And I'm led by the hand
With my head so full
Of problems and woe's
I feel so full
From my head to my toes
Someday soon it will be ok
The lady I'm seeing
Will make it all go away
Talking is the best
To a stranger it seems
I pour out my whole life
In buckets and reams
The time has now come
To forget all the past
To get up on my feet
And get off my ass

Swimming Pool

That holiday was great
There was nothing we can hate
The fun we had
When the sun shone down
Was the best ever, yet
As the day's rolled by, we all did sigh
As the holiday was seeing an end
The children cried, as they walked by my side
Nagging for more fun
The swimming pool just outside our door
Of the villa we did rent
Straight out the door the children ran
In their swimsuits
And me with a fan
I won't be a minute I said out loud
Wait until I get back
As I turned to walk away
Screams are then had
I turned back around and there I found
The youngest child I had
Floating in the open pool
A drawing was there to have
I dived in and tried to revive
My six-year-old, who had now died
Paramedics were on the scene
But no life can now be seen
I still love you Mum
I am not gone far
Get on with your life

And get that new car
Stop blaming yourself
It was my fault not you
I just didn't listen

Wonderful Mum

Mum I know your there
I feel your touch
I feel you're kiss
I can feel you everywhere
You were the best Mum to have
You're kindness was untrue
I wanted for nothing
You cheered me up
When I was blue
You taught me right from wrong
You raised me well for so long
Then you passed, and I'm so lost
Without you're love, beside us all
You will never be forgotten
You're love will always be
Caught up in my heart
It's there for all to see
I love you Mum

Acknowledgments

Thank you to Neil for teaching me how to put my poems in a folder ready to send.

April who put the poems in order and sorted out my manuscript for me.

Also to my husband Chris who always supports me whatever I'm doing, with all my crazy ways and nutty ideas.

Without them I wouldn't have got this far.

WS - #0178 - 060323 - C0 - 203/127/3 - PB - 9781913675318 - Matt Lamination